, and banish all the world

Jack Galmitz

ISBN: 978-81-8253-801-6

First Edition: 2021

Rs. 200/-

Cyberwit.net

HIG 45 Kaushambi Kunj, Kalindipuram

Allahabad - 211011 (U.P.) India

http://www.cyberwit.net

Tel: +(91) 9415091004

E-mail: info@cyberwit.net

Printed at VCORRE PRESS.

, and banish all the world

One

Announcement in the Daily Sentinel

[These are a few who didn't
extinguish self and enter bliss;
they are caught in the wheel
of birth, suffering, and death]

Avram Aaronson, Abe Abel, Darlene Adelman, Skip
"Tony" Adel, Lucille Adel, Marjorie Affortee, Mike
"Hammer" Agaloni, Geoffrey Appelbaum, Bobby
Axelrod, Herman Azor, Ruth Azor, Arthur Battucci,
Emily Best, Ernest Bestamo, Leonard Battista, Arnold
Bevelman, Heidi Borowitz, Francis Calhoun, Anthony
Caputo, Michael Chan, Kevin Chen, Carmel Corchcarin,
Steve Cohen, Jerry S. Cohn, A.G. Cooperman, Glen
Costello, Bob Crystal, Elliott Delaney, Kevin Delaney,
Sue Dougherty, Mervyn Douglas, Josh Drexler, Jobe
Drexler, David Eislitz, Peter Elhud, Lawrence Engel, Jr.,
Rondald Einziger, Angel Ephram, Craig Einhorn, Jeffrey
Erdheim, Fotis Fakatis, Mohammed Farouk, Bobby
Falco, Raymond Federman, Alexis Fix, Rupert Fox,
Angelina Fox, Mark Frazer, Mark Fulbright, Robert
Fuller, Anne Marie Fuller, Derek Fullmeister, Sean
Gavin, Sadie Geller, Issac Gellis, Sam Gellman, Itzak
Gilowitz, Jack Gitz, Leon Gittering, Michelle Gottlieb,
Adolphe Gottlieb, Frank Grant, Abagail Guzman,
Abdullah Ibrahim, Anwar Ibrahim, Kamal Ibrahim, Paul
Ingram, Sally Irving, Dan Ivey, Rebecca Irving, Albert
Isaacs, Irene Jacobs, Peter Jacobson, Ashish Jabara, Raj
Jalota, Beulah Jefferson, Beatrice Jefferson, Mirian
Jeffries, Geoffrey Jenkins, Al Johnson, Ralph Jones,
Sam Jones, Adam Johns, Gilbert Johnson, Tom Kaine,

Richard Kellman, Robert Kelly, John Kelly, Tom Kelly, Jr., Ann Kelly, Jorge Keuler, Santiago Keyser, Juan "Papi" Kili, Alex Killingsworth, John Koto, Kunihara Koto, Albert Kuhn, Alvin Kuhn, Nick Lane, Heidi "Baby" Lawrence, Kenneth Leaky, Chuck Lemming, June Leopold, Elizabeth Lilly, Jennifer Marks, Joshua Metzger, Steve Moore, Mark Mulaney, Thich Ng, Sandra Nissen, Anita Nunes, Laura Nussbaum, Mike O'Halloren, Johnny Ohare, Frank O'Hara, Craig Ott, John Pack, Mary Pack, Theodore Pagett, Andrew Palmer, Jane Pare, Melvin Pate, Raj Patel, Connell Peters, Amelia Peterson, Stephanie Pruitt, Danny Quinn, Reginald Quigley, Stewart Queen, Sally Raines, Jane Roberts, John Roberts, Amy Rudolph, Leon Russell, Abraham Sales, Roberta Sally, Harold Stanton, Wayne Stevens, Gerald Stuart, Edna Thomas, Dallas Thompson, Elvira Wallace, George Wallace, Evan Winchell, Eileen Yates, Al Zeigler, Patricia Zink

Impolite Nazis caused a traffic jam in downtown
Denver. Just when we thought we had returned to a
standard of behavior everyone agreed upon was normal,
American Nazis held a rally in Denver today and
swarmed the streets so that cars could not pass. Hardly
what had been agreed upon by 67% of the population.
There was brazen shouting beyond a line that that was
not meant to be crossed. "The people united will never
be defeated." "We must secure the existence of our
people and the future for white children." Back and forth
they shouted like opposing sides at a college football
game. In the end no one won. It grew dark. People
sauntered away.

When you suddenly realize that you can no longer whistle, your whole life flashes before your eyes. You ask yourself how that can be. You thought whistling was like riding a bike. You never forget how. So you panic and drink bottle after bottle of water thinking it is merely a mechanical thing. But as many times as you purse your wet lips and blow nothing comes out, not one whistling sound. You vaguely see yourself when you were young sitting on a bench whistling to a bird singing in a tree. You were certain that the bird responded to you and you to him. Your imitation of his calls was nearly perfect. So you ask yourself what happened in-between. What did you lose that has left you bereft of a scale of wind.

They took him into holding. He who had never used an eraser on a math problem. He was accused of feeling a cantaloupe just too many times. The produce clerk gave him up. Whispered his whereabouts to the 911 operator. And the cops arrived sooner than usual. They were on him in moments pressing their full weight and assumptions on his back up against the fruit stand as if he had already been charged and convicted. "Damn degenerates," one could be heard cursing. "I have children." In time, the cell began to fill with other men. He began to hear whispering and eventually it sounded like a teakettle left on the fire too long. If he looked over to see them, they turned away from him. He wanted to ask a policeman for his telephone call, but didn't dare.

He remembered I Was a Fugitive from a Chain Gang.

He looked around to see who might be his Sebastian T. Yale, but dropped it for the time being. He'd bide his time. His time would come and he'd make a break for it.

The wind makes the leaves more distinct and appealing than they were before its arrival. It relates the potted plants to the trees along the railroad and near and farther still. It shakes the sun settled on the beach ball that made its home by the shoreline. And much more. It parts the gathering storm of a boy's haircut. And there you are. Poised to move closer. The light is lifted from you and returned like a shaken bed cover. Everything about you moves in stasis. You'd think the world and its sudden objects had appeared out of nowhere. And they did. They did. It's right before you.

I like to think of dying as lying down in bed in striped
pajamas. The sheets are fresh and the pillow cases have
been aired out and smell of the sun. Birds lead to a skein
of new breath you can't forget. It is that soothing. You
can see tints of red in your mother's hair as she hangs the
laundry. She is younger than you remember. But you
climb the stairs anyway. You no longer have lung
disease or arthritis. You pass the sun. There are donkeys.
You smile. You love them. You run and the field keeps
lengthening. You never stop to ask why. You have let go
of the heavy sack you were carrying. You feel like a
bird, like breath.

My mother was the sea and I hadn't seen her in many years. When I finally reached the sand, I ran with my flip flops to her outstretched arms. She was tearful and sobbed. As did I. She asked me why I hadn't visited in such a long time and I explained that I had many things I had to undergo on dry land. She understood and patted me on the head. She waved me in and I put a cautious toe in the water. She scolded me and said after all these years the least I could do was jump in and frolic. So I sunk in and bobbed in her waves. "You feel so good mother. I had forgotten how comforting your embrace could be." "There. You see child."
I floated for a long time having discovered a newfound respect for my mother's largesse. Why she even fed the seagulls and all the slimy fish in her depths. She rejected nothing. And, I thought, isn't that just what a mother is supposed be.

Death lays down in the middle of the street and reaches a hand out to me like a beggar asking for change. "Don't you think I get tired," he says, "having to arrange all those mishaps and misadventures every hour?" I think about it briefly and say, "I imagine you would. Yes, sir." "So don't you think it is all right for me to rest a while?" "I think so, sir," I reply. "And just try to imagine how tiring it is having to use my imagination the way I do. Can you even conceive that?" "No, I can't." "All those cancer patients. All those dead by car bomb explosions. The heart failures." "It's an impressive list, sir." "Do you know what it took to create prison suicides. or death by stoning, or honor killings?" "I can't imagine what sort of imagination you must have to have thought out all those and the details that go with them." "Yes, the details are the thorny part."

I buried the hatchet in the backyard. I was certain that
over time wildflowers and shrubs and weeds would grow
on the spot and I would forget about it. It was a good
plan and one that should have worked.
Unbeknownst to me, hatchets, particularly hand-made
hatchets, grow offspring in the earth and set them forth
upon new scores to settle.
It was autumn and the brown leaves had fallen and
covered the grass. It was around Halloween. The sun had
set and the afterglow was upon the world. There was a
line of moving figures traveling out of the yard. I
couldn't tell if they were children in costumes or just
what they were.
The headdress of one or two of them slipped and sure
enough it revealed the head of a hatchet.
They marched out onto the street with a precision you
don't often see except in military maneuvers. They were
looking for neighbors, shopkeepers, any offenders,
anyone who had done me a disservice at one time or
another. I looked up powerless to stop what I had
begotten.

The Kung Fu Master had recently lost his wife to leukemia. They had been married for over 50 years and had had 8 children. The Master now lived with his one unmarried daughter.

The Master suddenly found himself striking objects whenever the impulse so moved him. It was a drastic change of personality. He had been studying the martial arts since he was 8 years old. He had never struck anyone or anything before.

Now, whenever his neighbors saw him on the street, they gave him wide berth. The greengrocer shoved his cart away as fast as he could when he saw him coming. The Master had recently, with one finger, plunged a deep hole into 3 watermelons.

When he was watching television with his daughter, she was terrified when he picked his nose: she was afraid he'd push too far up and puncture his brain.

Anyway, everyone was on the lookout for the Master now. The police were stationed in his neighborhood. There was just no telling whether he'd kick and uproot a fireplug or slash with his forearm and bend a traffic sign. People who owned cars began to park them in private lots, however costly.

One the day marking the one year anniversary of his wife's death, the Master was walking through his Lower East Side Neighborhood. A young girl happened to be at a corner he was approaching and when they were close to each other the girl reached out her hand and said, "Mister would you like some of my candy?"

"No thank you, little girl," the Master answered.

From that day on he was quiet inside, and sometimes at night alone in his bed he sobbed.

A man at work began to space out. His eyes were lusterless and unfocused much of the time. His coworkers thought it was a lack of sleep. Some spread rumors that he was on drugs. He stared at his computer screen enthralled by the colors rather than the text he was supposed to be deciphering. He almost entered the colors it was that intense a response.
In a corner of the office there was a leather couch for those who wanted to take short naps during the day. The man spent a great deal of time sleeping there. Office personnel said they could hear something like a purr when he lay down.
He licked his fingernails clean and then used his moist fingers to wipe his eyes and hair. No one was ever quite sure if he was really sleeping. Some swore they had seen an inner eyelid open when they approached him as silently as mice.

Here. In this spot in the clearing. You can see the
indentation in the earth where the marble base stood. As
to him, he left not a trace. I suppose that's what you'd
expect. There appear to be some hoof marks, but most
attribute that to deer crossings after the secluded space
had been abandoned. Some say they saw great
conflagrations when he was said to have touched down
on the earth, but I don't believe it. I'm not a man of faith.
I like hard evidence and there is none.
It might have been the toasters. The flames, I mean. You
know he was the Provider of Toasters to all new
customers or devotees, as they called them. He was said
to have a jack in his person and he could demonstrate
how well the toasters worked right in this nature temple
of his. They were industrial toasters, of course. Not your
usual home toasters. And you ask yourself is that why he
was worshipped and I say it just might have been the
reason. Yes.
I have my own toasters, if you're interested. Have them
in the wagon . I can show you one if you'd like. No.
Well, okay. No harm in my asking is there?

The elephant shifted in the chair and put down his glass
of iced tea. He put his two front feet over his eyes and I
could see his chest heaving as he tried to hold back his
tears.

"He was such a good friend. He never harmed anything,"
he said in a broken voice.

"I found him in a clearing with half his face sawed off.
Half his face gone," and at that he started to cry.

I didn't know what to say. There was really nothing I
could say to comfort him. What could I say?

The young man found it harder and harder to shake
hands with people he was introduced to. Everyone now
had blades sticking out of their palms. It was impossible
to touch people without serious injury.
The young man reminisced about a time in his past when
people had soft hands, soft fleshy hands and the hands
were warm.
He looked over his own hands and they were just as they
had been when he was a boy. Perhaps, he thought, it was
because he petted his cats so often.
In school, the boys no longer had thumb fights or arm
wrestled. They scratched their wooden desks and
sometimes the chalk board with their hands.
There was a girl in the young man's class who was
demure. He noticed that she wore gloves to school,
something no one else did. He decided he's wanted to
know her better.
They began to walk home together after school. They
were both shy, so they didn't say much. They would just
say goodbye when they reached the girl's house.
After months of courting, one day the boy reached out
his hand and the girl let him hold hers. She gave herself
to him. It was the start of something, something very old
and very new.

A man had a wife who simply had to have a bidet
replace their perfectly functioning toilet bowl. The
package with the bidet attachment arrived on a Sunday.
While his wife was ripping open the box and reading
instructions which he knew she could not possibly
understand, he did a quick search on the internet about
installing such a thing. The first thing was the water had
to be shut off in the apartment. He looked at their toilet
and it did not have a nozzle to shut off the water supply.
He decided to take a walk believing for the moment that
his wife was at least smart enough to realize that she
could do nothing without shutting off the water. He
hoped she would shut the water off in the basement or
else do the wise thing and hire someone to install the
bidet.
He went out. He was sitting on a bench when it occurred
to him to cut short the excursion and hurry home lest his
wife did something ruinous to the apartment and those
below it.
Sure enough when he opened the door there was a pond
on the living room granite tiles and spreading out to the
bedroom rugs.
He went onto their deck and took out the rubber raft. He
got in and paddled to the bedroom, removed his books
from their shelf and put them in a knapsack. He left
behind his wife screaming as she tried to hold back the
stream of water coming from the pipe in the bathroom
wall.

The worm called me from the ground. It was hard to
make out what he was saying. It was like we were on the
phone and had a bad connection. But I finally understood
him to say please mister pick me up off the ground. It
rained and I'm drowning. Please.
Well, it was pretty hard to just deny a dying worm's
wish, so I picked him up and put him in my shirt pocket.
He didn't thank me, but importuned that I grab some soil,
too, as he would need that to live in and to help dry off
his saturated pores. It was a request for something
beyond the ordinary, but I relented and scooped up some
earth and put that in my pocket, too.
When we got home, I took out an old goldfish bowl from
the closet and put in the soil and then the worm. He was
delighted. We talked a lot now and the connection was
clear. We shared worldviews and it was pleasant to have
a friend with like ideas.
I brought home fresh earth everyday so he would have
nourishment. He grew so much from eating that I had to
keep buying larger tanks for him. He began to develop
features and appendages.
One day I came home and he was not in his tank. I
looked around frantically. I found a beautiful woman
wearing a sheer nightgown in my bed. She rolled around
to give me a full view. Then it struck me: the worm
turned.

The aliens had assimilated in the neighborhood so well
that if it were not for their elongated faces you couldn't
tell the difference between them and humans. They went
to the local diner mornings for breakfast specials and
tipped 15% or more. Some of the males wore cowboy
hats where appropriate. They wore blue jeans: Wrangler
and Levis.
They drove cars imported from Japan or Germany. They
owned homes where they raised families. Many had
joined local churches and sang hymns on Sunday
mornings.
It looked like things would work out wonderfully until a
young woman started to date an alien. Heads turned
when they walked down Main Street holding hands. If
they kissed in the movie theater the sound of snarls and
hisses rose to the chandeliers.
Eventually, the young couple applied for a marriage
license. The clerk wouldn't grant it. The humans held a
town meeting soon after. It was unanimously agreed that
humans and aliens could not marry. A town ordinance
was passed to that effect.
The couple took the ordinance to court. The ordinance
was temporarily blocked. The suit went all the way to
the Supreme Court. While Loving v Virginia seemed
good precedent, the conservatives on the Court said the
fact that the alien in this case was not human meant that
Loving did not hold and disallowed the marriage. A call
for Congress to take action soon arouse in the major
cities. There was great discontent in the land.

Christmas morning the family was surprised to find bow
and arrow sets under the tree for everyone. The father
had a plan and he saw no reason to let religion stand in
the way of its achievement. Times had become hard and
it was now necessary to do whatever it took to survive.
After eating a hearty breakfast of Dutch baby pancakes
and roasted plums, they dressed and went out in the cold.
"We'll start with squirrels," the father said. "They're most
plentiful."
So with bows in hand and quivers ready, they scattered
down the block looking up at the Norway maple trees.
The pickings were small at this time of year and the one
shot the mother got off went all awry.
"Squirrels are very nimble," she said.
They graduated to stray cats. It being dead of winter,
they knew the cats often hid on the wheels of parked cars
to get out of the wind. They snuck up in teams to the cars
and one of the group banged on the hood. The children
came close to striking a cat or two, but in the end this
idea failed, too.
"All right. This is a last resort," said the father. Every
moment of every day there are all these noisy,
obnoxious, poorly dressed people walking by our house.
We have to do what we have to do."
All chimed in with father.

A man had grown completely bald. Like most with his condition, his head shone in the sun. It was, in its fashion, a badge of sorts.

The man enjoyed walks in the woods and sometimes climbing mountain paths. One day he decided to go for an all day climb.

He was dressed for it: he had the boots, climber pants, a hiking pole, and a sense of élan vital.

He took a bus upstate where the mountains were taller than those near his home. It was a pleasant drive and he took advantage of his window seat as it was deep in autumn and the leaves had reached their peak of fall colors.

When he arrived, he simply took a path up one of the mountains. It wasn't too steep to begin with, although as he progressed the angle up was enough to make breathing a bit difficult.

He climbed with determination. He looked out at the valley below sometimes when he rested and breathed a sigh of satisfaction. He could even see the peak of the mountain and the cragginess of the rocks up there.

As he drew nearer to the top, an eagle circled him. She seemed frantic, as if one of her young with its bald head had fallen from the nest. She dove down on the man.

He froze and fell backwards to the earth. The eagle had her mouth full of carrion and with her talons she opened the man's mouth and vomited up the carrion into his. When he swallowed, she again gorged him with more carrion.

When she was satisfied that her lost young one was sated, she flew up to the nest to feed the rest of the hatchlings.

After the ordeal, the man snuck down the mountain. He decided from that moment on that he had to buy a toupee. Never mind what others thought.

Two

It was a school trip to the zoo and a group of boys ran into the Great Ape House. There was one giant upland gorilla in a cage sitting quietly, contemplatively in the corner. Every now and then he reached for some scraps of vegetables on the floor left from the last feeding. The boys started to bait him. The ape had a huge crowned head and the boys called him bonehead. They yelled "fat lazy slob" and "dummy" and whatever hurtful words they could think of. The ape seemed to be unaware of them. He looked forward and kept a stately composure. Even some adults in the room tittered.

Suddenly, the ape pursed his lower lip and opened his mouth and spewed his saliva evenly on the boys who were lined up along a rail in front of the cage. When they realized what happened, they ran out screaming as if they had been sprayed with acid.

In the meantime, the ape had turned to face the wall, his back revealing a stunning hair shade of silver.

A little girl named Mabel wore her hair in cornrows. Her mother took hours at night doing her daughter's hair for school the next day. Mabel was a good and obedient student and loved school.
The desks were old-fashioned wooden desks that were bolted into the floor. Some students put their chewed gum under the desks. Others used penknives to carve hearts with their initials and a girl's initials they were fond of into the desktop.
The desks were in rows and behind Mabel sat a feral pig named Albert. Because Mabel's hair was in cornrows, he just couldn't resist and began to nibble on her hair. He was a huge pig and eventually he chewed down to her scalp, which caused her to bleed.
She touched her head and when she saw blood on her hand she began to cry out loud. She was inconsolable. When the teacher saw the blood on Mabel's hand she called another student and told her to immediately accompany Mabel to the school nurse's office.
"And as for you, Albert, you pig, you are to write 'I will not eat girls' cornrows ever again for as long as I live'
"and you are to write this 5000 times in your notebook as punishment tonight."

Dear Lucinda:

When you return from work, you'll find I'm not at home.
I've decided to go on a short trip. I'm not sure where I'm
headed, but don't worry. Everything is fine.
I've left you food in the refrigerator. It's mostly offal:
chicken livers, hearts, cow's intestines, and pig's ears.
You can get recipes off the internet, so enjoy!
If you don't want animal organs, there's ribs in the
refrigerator, and pork belly, oxtail, ham hocks, Canadian
bacon, and much more.
And don't mind the seared section of the rug. I sacrificed
a virgin this morning and then set up a funeral pyre and
burned her remains. You won't find anything but ashes
and, as I mentioned, a burn mark on the rug. We can
discuss whether to have the rug cleaned or whether to
consider a different floor covering when I get back.
Sorry about bringing Buddy with me, but I wanted the
company. I know how much you look forward to him
greeting you at the door when you get home and
scratching his paws against your breasts.
Speaking of which, please take care of those breasts and
keep them as pert as ever.
You know how much I look forward to them staring at
me when you remove your bra at bedtime.

Your loving husband,
Elbert

A man took his wife and three children on a trip up North. They drove on winding roads by mountainsides and the man pointed out some of the sites to his children who sat in the back seat of the car. It was autumn and the children were mildly interested in the reflections of the fall leaves in the larger lakes in the valley below. Mostly they were engaged in playing games on their tablets and didn't want to be bothered.

After hours of driving, the man was began to feel stiff. He looked around for a place to pull off the road and stretch his legs. Before long he found a site designated by the Thruway Authority as a scenic view and he pulled the car in the space and parked.

He walked around a bit and stretched his arms. Then he went to the edge of the cliff and admired the view of one of the oldest towns in the state. It looked grand surrounded by the fall foliage.

He called the kids to come and look. They exchanged meaningful looks with each other and made annoyed faces. Their looks did not go unnoticed.

The father called over his boys. They dragged their feet and pulled more faces.

He grabbed one of his sons and in an instant tossed him down the mountainside.

"Wow," he said to the rest of the family. "Wasn't that an amazing sight?"

A man who lived alone often consulted the Magic 8 Ball
for life's more pressing questions. He'd had it since he
was a boy and it never let him down. He had once been
in love, but when he considered popping the most
important question in a man's life, he first asked the
Magic 8 Ball and it answered "definitely not." So he
remained a bachelor his entire life.
The Magic 8 Ball had steered him to his rent controlled
apartment by the waterfront. He had saved a great deal of
money over his lifetime because of this advice. The
Magic 8 Ball had chosen for him the minimalist interior
design of his home. He still enjoyed being in his
apartment because of the sparsely decorated rooms.
He had enjoyed a life of painting rather than
photography as a result of consulting the 8 Ball. He had
enjoyed all the masterpieces of film because of the
directions of the Magic 8 Ball. His friends, the bars he
went to, the clothes he wore were all decided by the ball.
It would not be a far reach to say the Magic 8 Ball had
essentially been the one and only guide through his life.
When he fell ill late in life, he asked the Magic 8 Ball
one fateful question: it told him to be cremated and have
his ashes scattered rather than be buried in a cemetery.
He had hospice care in his home. Amid all the comings
and goings of nurses and assistants, the man continued to
ask the Magic 8 Ball everything that concerned him. He
even asked the ultimate question: will there be a God
there when I die? The Magic 8 Ball gave a vague reply:
it's too early to tell.
One sunny day, the man happened to look at the
window. On the sill he saw a pigeon walking back and

forth. He was struck as if by a hammer blow. "That's it!"
he cried. "That's it!"

The man's wife sang from the moment she woke up till after he went to sleep. She was a member a group of seniors who sang karaoke songs. Since the pandemic, the group shared their songs by way of Skype.

The wife took her performances very seriously. She had a notebook filled with her set list. She had a larger repertoire than any of the other members according to her.

The problem was the wife simply couldn't stay in tune in many of her renditions of popular songs. She was so so, but she would invariably hit a note so off key that the husband in his adjoining room would begin to grind his teeth.

He ordered a pitch pipe, an expensive one, and when it was delivered he demonstrated to his wife how to use it. He reminded her to always be sure that her voice remained in the same pitch throughout the song she was singing.

Needless to say, after the demonstration, his wife returned to her room and computer and never used the pitch pipe again.

The man returned to grinding his teeth.

Then one day, he felt something stuck in his throat. He was afraid he would choke to death if he didn't get out what was stuck. He reached deep down his throat and pulled out a white rabbit. And he managed this without a wand or top hat.

He brought the rabbit to show his wife and explained to her what had happened. But just as she listened to his explanation of how to use the pitch pipe to improve her singing, so she listened attentively to his explanation of how he had pulled a rabbit out of his mouth. When he was finished speaking, she returned to singing her songs off key.

As for the man, he eventually ground his teeth down to stumps and shared lettuce with his rabbit.

In midtown in broad daylight, two mouths were yelling at each other. "I know what you did," said the mouth with red lipstick. "How could you?" taunted the mouth with clear lip gloss. "You're just a mouth. "I have my ways," retorted the wide open mouth with red lipstick. "I hear things," said the mouth with red lipstick. "You have no ears you idiot," said the mouth with clear lip gloss.

"I have informants. They pass information to me through my taste buds. So there," shouted the mouth with red lipstick.

As the arguing heated up, the mouth with red lipstick suddenly bit the mouth with clear lip gloss. It drew blood.

The crowd that had gathered sighed a loud "oh" in response to the spiraling into violence. Someone called 911.

A policeman on his beat arrived. He put out his hands and separated the two mouths. "What's going on here?" he demanded.

The overwrought mouth with clear lip gloss cried, "she bit my lip and it's bleeding." "Is that right?" asked the policeman. "She was causing me emotional distress," retorted the mouth with red lipstick.

"Look, I'll have to run you both in unless you both calm down. Can you do that for me? Can we have a civil discourse here?"

It was their first date. They were both performance
artists and had been introduced by a mutual friend. The
man wanted to impress the woman so he got reservations
at Mimi's, an atmospheric French restaurant in the
Village. She wanted to impress him, too, so she spent the
day with a friend who was a painter.

What made the time she spent with her friend the painter
special was that she had him paint a sexy outfit directly
on her body. It was such an excellent job that when the
man and woman met outside the restaurant, the man had
no idea his date was not wearing an enchanting black
dinner dress.

The two hit it off. Dinner was fabulous. Their
conversation was scintillating. They ordered a second
bottle of Bordeaux and topped it off with pastries and
espressos.

When they got outside, it was raining hard. The
restaurant was on a small side street and it was going to
be difficult to get a taxi. They stood holding each other
around their waists and looked on the rain jumping on
the cobblestones.

The man looked over at his date and saw her dress was
beginning to run off of her body. Her breasts were bare
and the flesh was more pronounced because around them
a portion of what had appeared to be a black dress still
clung to her. He could see her shaved pubis under the
tiny lights strung on the awning.

"Oh" was all he said before he was a dog on all fours and
mounting her from behind.

www.ingramcontent.com/pod-product-compliance
Lightning Source LLC
LaVergne TN
LVHW041805190726
843493LV00008B/2795